Foreword

Overstrand and Sidestrand were two peaceful villages in the spring of 1883. By the end of that year an invasion had been begun. This booklet attempts to tell the story of that invasion, the 'Poppyland' story.

In writing this booklet the authors have made constant reference to cuttings from the local newspapers. The regularity with which 'Poppyland' is mentioned and the interest it always generates in the letter columns made us realise that the story needed telling in a fuller version. The beginning of the events described has now passed from living memory, and even the 'Garden of Sleep' is almost a lifetime away. As we mention in the text, 'Poppyland' is now in the realm of legend. In telling the story we felt it important to try to return to original sources for information and avoid what could not be verified. Legends are usually based on fact but a gloss is added in the course of time, and our aim is to be as factual as possible.

Thus we wrote in the foreword to the first edition, twenty years ago. The comments still stand, but what a resurgence of interest the intervening period has produced! And now a fourth edition is required. As ever, our thanks are extended to all who have assisted in gathering material for this booklet, to those who have told individual stories, for guidance with library and museum material, for help with photographs, and most of all for access to the collection of Gwen Parry, whose ambition was always to retell the story. If you enjoy this booklet and would like to further capture the flavour of this part of North Norfolk in late Victorian times, may we suggest our companion book *Poppyland in Pictures*, compiled by Elizabeth Jones.

David Cleveland, Peter Stibbons

A discovery

On 30th August 1883, readers of the *Daily Telegraph* opened their early morning paper to the usual mixture of news and opinion. On an inside page was the sports news with Dr W. G. Grace being selected for the 'South' cricket team to play the 'North', and Highland Chief heading the betting for the St Leger. On the same page an irate letter-writer, signing himself *Pedes*, complained at having to pay a shilling for the first two miles of a cab journey, and beneath several other letters on the 'exorbitant' cost of travelling by cab was a brief report concerning a man who set fire to his wife. Heading the page and filling a column and a quarter with fine and uncomfortable print, was a column titled 'Poppyland', with the by-line 'By a Holidaymaker' and written 'At a Farmhouse by the Sea'.

For those who took the trouble to read the article it proved to be a description of what was then a quiet corner of rural England. The article was to be the first of a series about East Anglia, and North Norfolk in particular, that was to change the area to the extent that ten years later the same writer was to lament over what he was first to popularise. The writer of the article was Clement Scott.

The Great Eastern Railway had reached Cromer in 1877. No doubt the railway company encouraged journalists to make use of their facilities and Clement Scott had taken up the opportunity. The first article did not mention towns or villages by name, but the story begins as, having arrived at Cromer, he finds no place to stay.

> I turned my back on perhaps the prettiest watering place of the East Coast and walked along the cliffs. At a mile removed from the seaside town I had left I did not find a human being. There they all were below me, as I rested amongst the fern on Lighthouse Cliff, digging on the sands, playing lawn tennis, working, reading, flirting and donkey-riding. In that red-roofed town,

The jetty at Cromer in Scott's time, when it was the rule to 'crowd upon the little pier at night'

the centre of all that was fashionable and select, there was not a bed to be had for love or money; all home comforts, all conveniences to which well-bred people had been inured were deliberately sacrificed for the sake of a lodging amongst a little society that loved its band, its pier, its shingle and its sea. Custom had established a certain rule at this pretty little watering place and it was religiously obeyed; it was the rule to go on the sands during the morning, to walk on one cliff for a mile in the afternoon, to take another mile in the opposite direction at sunset, and to crowd upon the little pier at night.

Such was the impression he conveyed of Cromer. In the context of this first 'Poppyland' article it is a pleasant enough description but merely a preliminary to what he was to discover. In fact, a quarter of the total article had already been used before he commented on his arrival at Cromer, to eulogise on other places he had visited, particularly those overseas in Europe. Perhaps if Cromer had been able to offer a bed for the night his article would have been written there, the train caught back to London the next day and 'Poppyland' never created. As it was, he walked on, following the cliff-top paths.

Not desiring to be followed I strolled on and, attracted by a ruined church tower, took a cut through the cornfields towards a cluster of farms and a distant village. It is difficult to convey an idea of the silence of the fields through which I passed, or the beauty of the prospect that surrounded me – a blue sky without a cloud across it; a sea sparkling under a haze of heat; wild flowers in profusion around me, poppies predominating everywhere. So great was the change from the bustle of fashion to the unbroken quiet that I could scarcely believe that I was only parted by a dip of coastline from music and laughter and seaside merriment, from bands and bathing machines from croquet and circulating libraries.

Scott walked on, passing through the tiny fishing village of Overstrand where children just out of school were the only sign of life. Continuing along the meandering road he left the village behind.

At last my patience was rewarded. Half a mile beyond the deserted village, at a bend of the road under the shadow of a windmill, there was presented to my sight what appeared to be a very cosy spot. It was one of those farm-houses which is an exact representation of the cottage that all children are set to draw when they begin their first lesson. A little red-brick house with three white windows on the first-floor, a little white door in the middle, a window at either side, and a stack of chimneys at each end of the cottage.

Mill House, where Scott and Louie Jermy met, and where Scott was to stay on many occasions. Miller Jermy is by the door.

The house was divided from the road by a white gate and palings, and in front of it was a garden brilliant with flowers . . . This was evidently the miller's house.

Scott knocked at the door and his enquiry whether he could be allowed lodging for a few days was met with the reply, 'Indeed you could.' It came from the miller's daughter and she, together with the house, village and surrounding countryside, entered into the legend that became 'Poppyland'.

The Garden of Sleep

All legends are a mixture of fact and fantasy, accuracy and hearsay, developed in the course of time. 'Poppyland' is no exception and many stories have grown up that are difficult to substantiate. One fact that cannot be denied is that at the centre of the story was 'The Garden of Sleep'.

Continuing east from Overstrand and the miller's cottage, the road wound again towards the north. Today all that remains of what was once the 'main' road is Tower Lane. At the top, the road bent back in a hairpin and ran through what are now the grounds of Sidestrand Hall. The original line of the road cannot be traced, for the bend of the hairpin is no longer there; Tower Lane ends abruptly at the edge of the cliff. When Scott walked the road he was met at the bend by the sight of a tower standing some three hundred yards away. This structure was to feature in many of his writings and must have made a considerable impact on him when he first saw it. It was a tower without a church, already by Scott's time perched precariously at the cliff's edge. Around it were the graves of the villagers of Sidestrand with, once again, the poppies in evidence. In Scott's imaginative and fanciful mind stories and verses grew over the coming months and years.

What was this mysterious building? It was in fact a tower that had had its church removed. St Michael's Church, Sidestrand, had been built on this site early in the 14th century. Its original tower had stood until 1841 when it is said to have fallen on a stormy night.

James Craske, a bricklayer of Overstrand, was given the task of rebuilding it. He com-

The tower in the 'Garden of Sleep'

pleted in 1848 a round tower that barely reached the height of the nave and which certainly did not match the rest of the church. It did, however, serve to house the bell that was supplied by one Thomas Hurry. Craske's bill was £45, and Hurry's £15 2s; the account being met by a one shilling rate that brought in £62 2s 4½d.

The collapse of the original tower served to make Samuel Hoare III, the local landowner, and his brother-in-law, Sir Thomas Fowell Buxton, together with others, consider the possibility of removing St Michael's further inland, as it was obvious that cliff erosion would eventually lead to its demise. They commenced a fund for this purpose, and raised £300, which was invested at three per cent. By 1880, long after these two initiators were dead, it was decided to implement the plan. Sir Samuel Hoare V, then living at Sidestrand Hall, gave some land and added most of the other funds needed, and the church was moved, stone by stone, to its present site. The last service in the church on the cliff top was held at Christmas 1880 and the newly erected church dedicated and blessed on 29th September 1881. To it had been added a new tower, more in keeping with the original, and thus Craske's tower was left on the cliff top.

'The Garden of Sleep' was the name Scott gave to the tower, its graveyard and, with the sub-title of 'A Summer Song', his best remembered verses.

> On the grass of the cliff, at the edge of the steep,
> God planted a garden - a garden of sleep!
> 'Neath the blue of the sky, in the green of the corn,
> It is there that the royal red poppies are born!
> Brief days of desire, and long dreams of delight,
> They are mine when my Poppy-Land cometh in sight.
> In music of distance, with eyes that are wet,
> It is there I remember and there I forget!
> O! heart of my heart! where the poppies are born,
> I am waiting for thee, in the hush of the corn.
> Sleep! Sleep!
> From the Cliff to the Deep!
> Sleep, my Poppy-land,
> Sleep!
>
> In my garden of sleep, where red poppies are spread,
> I wait for the living alone with the dead.
> For a tower in ruins stands guard o'er the deep,
> At whose feet are green graves of dear women asleep!
> Did they love, as I love, when they lived by the sea?
> Did they wait, as I wait, for the days that may be?
> Was it hope or fulfilling, that entered each breast,

Sidestrand church:

Top: before the first tower fell.

Centre: With Craske's tower, to be left when the church was moved.

Bottom: Removed to its present site.

Ere death gave release, and the poppies gave rest?
O! life of my life! on the cliffs by the sea,
By the graves in the grass, I am waiting for thee!
Sleep! Sleep!
In the Dews by the Deep!
Sleep, my Poppy-land,
Sleep!

It is difficult to put a date on these verses, but the earliest that has come to light at present is July 1885. They soon became available in many other forms. Isodore de Lara put a melody to the verses and Chappell and Sons published the music. Postcards of the tower often carried the verses, and a compilation of the articles of Scott about Poppyland opened with 'The Garden of Sleep'. But the poem itself was not all. The tower and garden were to appear in many of Scott's other writings.

Time precludes mention of every instance, even if it were possible to track down all the allusions. Suffice it to take the first story, 'Madonna Mia', which appears in the 1884 *Theatre Annual*. Scott, as we shall mention again later, was

The central characters in the story: London critic and travel writer Clement Scott, and miller's daughter Louie Jermy

editor of the *Theatre* magazine, and also a considerable contributor, with many poems, written apparently to fill odd spaces, bearing his initials. In this particular, rather lengthier, story, we find an 'odd, erratic, unconventional creature, Lancelot Dashwood'. He is a 'barrister, writer, journalist and dramatist . . . supposed to be bound hand and foot to London'. He has discovered a place by the name of 'Mill Farm' when visiting Norfolk the previous August, it now being Christmas, and 'within a short distance of the Mill Farm, and close to the edge of the crumbling cliff, was a deserted churchyard and a ruined church-tower'. He is attracted by poppies, cornfields and a picture of a woman at Mill Farm. He learns from 'the little maiden of the farm', by name Hesba, that the woman often visits Mill Farm and back in London he chances to meet her. They are married and happy, happiest when at the Farm, until she is drawn, when there, to a visiting actor. Left alone, Dashwood broods, sitting on a tombstone by the deserted tower, and it is while there that his wife returns to him. 'She had prayed and prevailed. But a shadow had passed over two lives; and a chill struck two hearts that had deeply loved.'

We will take our second example of a 'Poppyland' story from an *Illustrated London News* of 1885. 'Come Back to Me', a 'Story of the Sea', begins on Christmas Eve when Maida, the daughter of old Starling, of the Mill Farm, brings news of a wreck. A vessel has been driven down the coast, the Sheringham lifeboatmen, Cromer rocket brigade and Overstrand fishermen have stood by to help but she is driven ashore at Sidestrand, where waits Maida, who 'would have been the Grace Darling . . . a second Florence Nightingale'.

Some years before, she had parted from her love, Frederick Moore, 'in the churchyard, under the solitary grey tower'. It is at the base of the cliff below that the vessel is driven ashore and the rocket brigade is able to fire a life-saving line. Maida's father cries that she must not be allowed to see one of the bodies brought ashore, and it is carried into the tower. He later tells her that it is Frederick and she determines to see him, only to find on reaching the tower that a mistake has been made and that Frederick has been brought ashore alive!

Such was the melodramatic style, which Scott added to the background material he used. Sometimes, as in the first story, he did not reveal the place about which he wrote; at other times, as in the second instance, he placed it by naming the towns and villages. Always he reveals his romanticism, often wandering round and round an idea before actually coming to the point.

Clement Scott – Londoner

Who, then, was Clement Scott? Was he the Laurence Dashwood of 'Madonna Mia'? Was he 'chained to London by the unbreakable fetters of the world, associated with it by countless ties and interests; a man well known and not altogether disliked, a man whose cares and anxieties were incessant'? Was he the man whose 'countless occupations made his summer holidays brief enough', but who 'on one occasion fate presented just the little refuge he so much desired'?

Clement Scott had been born the son of William Scott, Vicar of Christ Church, Hoxton, in London, on 6th October 1841. He attended a private school in Islington prior to seven years at Marlborough College, developing in his youth a liking for the dramatic arts. He described himself in his early days as a 'strange, rather silent, introspective and thoughtful boy' but by the time he was twenty-one he was bold enough to offer to undertake literary readings to various societies, commencing with the Great Western Railway Literary Society. Before embarking on an outline of his literary and dramatic career we ought to mention, though he strangely makes no claim for it himself in his autobiographical writing, that he is credited with playing, in 1874, the first game of lawn tennis, together with Major Wingfield, the inventor, Alfred Thompson and Alfred Lubbock.

His great achievements, however, were to be in the field of dramatic criticism. He visited the theatre when home from Marlborough and at school debated on theatrical topics. His father was an avid writer, chiefly for the *Morning Chronicle* and the *Saturday Review*. Clement became a clerk at the War Office, where he was a friend of the son of Thomas Hood, the poet, and by young Tom he was encouraged in his efforts to become a critic. Membership of the Arundel Club introduced him to bohemian society and he began enthusiastically his first appointment as drama critic for the *Victoria Review*. After a while he pursued the matter of payment for his work and was told the periodical was likely to close for lack of funds. Anxious to assist, Scott handed over twenty pounds, only to find both the *Victoria Review* and its editor disappear. Undeterred, he continued writing and on hearing that the *Sunday Times* drama critic was retiring, arranged a number of testimonials from influential people, especially those associated with his father, and obtained the post. His first assignment was to describe a tournament, which he says he did by writing a column and a half where a few lines might be expected. Thus Scott began a style of criticism which he can justifiably claim to have originated.

He was favourably disposed towards French theatre; in fact one might say he was a rebel and innovator in that a body of opinion felt that the British theatre was for British actors and playwrights alone. Scott's standing up for what was good in French theatre led to his dismissal from the *Sunday Times*.

He was able to adopt the title 'Almaviva' when working later for the *London Figaro* where, in spite of lawsuits over what he wrote, he had the editor's support. Scott was unpopular with audiences for criticising booing and hissing on the first nights of productions, and with management, because he insisted on first night reviews. He stuck to his opinions and next took up a position with the *Telegraph*, in which he was to wield great power in the theatre for nearly three decades.

He was invited to write for the *Daily Telegraph* in 1871, continuing for two years with the *Observer* as well. He had also continued at the War Office and was to do so until 1879, but then he committed himself totally to his writing. He undertook a wide range of tasks with theatrical articles, book reviews, anonymous letters to begin controversies, biographies, coverage of most major events and, of particular interest to us, holiday articles. These began with 'On a Car through Connemara' which he describes as 'the first of my series of descriptive holiday articles by land and lake and "poppyland" and sea'. The particular mention of 'Poppyland' seems again to indicate the important part it played in his life, writing the above sentence as he does at the close of his career.

The *Theatre* magazine that we have already mentioned was Scott's editorial responsibility from 1880 to 1889. It was a

As a theatre critic, Clement Scott's circle of friends included many actors who came to visit Overstrand.

monthly periodical with an annual as well, and in addition to many of the articles he frequently wrote verses to fill up the pages. It may well be that 'The Garden of Sleep' first appeared as one of these verses; the introduction of Scott's *Some Notable Hamlets* makes such an attribution. His verses appear also in the collection *Lays of a Londoner* and in *Poems for Recitation* and *Lays and Lyrics*. Scott also ventured, without receiving much lasting acclaim, into the field of writing plays himself, though he mainly confined himself to making adaptations from French plays.

The 'Poppyland' literature we will deal with later in the story; suffice to mention here that his writings were collected and published in a series of books; for example *Round about the Islands* (1874), *Sisters by the Sea* (1897), *Among the Apple Orchards* (1894) and *Poppy-land* itself (1885). One of his articles, entitled 'Lazyland', concerns the area of Suffolk around Yoxford. Writing for the *Telegraph*, this time in 1890, he eulogises again on rural solitude and peace, white gates and latticed windows, and the variety of destinations that can be reached with the assistance of the Great Eastern Railway Company! It is perhaps fortunate that the name 'Lazyland' did not acquire the same currency that 'Poppyland' did!

This article, as with most of Scott's articles concerning travel in Great Britain, spends a good deal of time making comparisons with continental resorts and pleasures. He draws on his experience of Rhine boats and Norway steamers, of the view from the Rigli or sunrise over Lake Lucerne. He was indeed a widely travelled man. He journeyed to Chicago to visit the World Fair and continued around the world visiting San Francisco, Tokyo, Canton, Shanghai, Bombay and other major cities, which resulted in *Pictures of the World*, published in 1894. He was a contributor in later years to the *New York Herald* and he took up a full-time post with the *Herald* in 1899 when he left the *Telegraph* to go to New York. Evidently, however, the post was not mutually satisfactory as we find him back in London in 1901 founding a new penny weekly, the *Free Lance*. This was not a success and after a long illness Scott died on 25th June 1904, and was laid to rest in the chapel of the Sisters of Nazareth at Southend. He had written in one of his early articles about a 'Nazareth House' at Hammersmith, run by the 'Sisters of a Catholic order' and Scott may have had some connection with this order.

Married twice, he had six children by his first wife, Isobel du Maurier, and while two sons died in infancy, the other two sons and two daughters established themselves in successful military and artistic careers. The children and grandchildren recall a family game which throws some light on their father, involving them meeting and trying to guess where he was this time! His second wife was Constance Margarite Brandon, herself a journalist.

Scott and his influence

We must return to Clement Scott's prime occupation of theatrical criticism and see where and how Overstrand and Sidestrand were to be influenced by him. The introduction to Scott's compilation *Some Notable Hamlets* describes Scott as 'the most popular and influential dramatic critic in the greatest city in the world for more than thirty years'. The *National Biographical Dictionary* describes him as 'the pioneer of picturesque style of dramatic criticism'. It also states the opinion that Scott's habit of mind was neither impartial nor judicial, and while he was in the forefront of the development of the theatre in his early years, he reacted strongly against developments at the end of the century, particularly against the school of drama led by Ibsen. Scott describes his *Ghosts* as 'a loathsome sore unbandaged', 'an open drain', 'a dirty act done publicly' and 'a lazar-house with all its doors and windows open'. George Bernard Shaw reacted on behalf of the modern school with a play entitled *Widowers' Houses*, aimed at Scott.

It was natural then that a man who was prepared to be so damning could be very unpopular, but also much appreciated by those whom he praised, which praise could be full to overflowing. In the van of the revival of the theatre were the Bancrofts, Squire and Marie, the actor-managers of the Prince of Wales Theatre. Scott helped adapt a French play for them under the title *Diplomacy* – parodied elsewhere as 'Diplunacy' – and numbered them among his friends. Ellen Terry was perhaps the leading female actress of the time and Scott frequently wrote in her praise. Wilson Barrett of the Princess Theatre, Beerbohm Tree who built Her Majesty's, and George Alexander of St James's are all amongst those actor-managers whom Scott praised on many occasions. Perhaps the greatest praise was reserved for that doyen of the Victorian stage, Henry Irving, particularly in Scott's book *Some Notable Hamlets*. Such was the society in which Scott moved, and of such were the people who came to 'Poppyland' because of the influence of Scott.

Theodore Watts, later Watts-Dunton, was one of the first to visit. He was caring for the poet Algernon Swinburne, whose behaviour had become eccentric to the point that he was described as 'the most talked about man in England'. His collected poems run to eleven volumes, and the *Dictionary of National Biography* records that his 'summer holidays, usually spent at the seaside with his insepara-ble friend, were the sources of much lyrical verse'. Amongst those lines linked with Overstrand we find again the poppies.

> Steep and deep and sterile, under fields no plough can tame,
> Dip the cliffs, full-fledged with poppies red as love or shame.

Clara Watts-Dunton recalled that although she was not there herself until later years, her husband vividly remembered the tearing of the earth when sections of the land slipped into the sea, and earlier events at Mill House.

Robert Reece, Henry Petit, Hayden Coffin and John Hare were other prom-inent actors who visited Poppyland. Many of the happenings were evidently of a riotous nature. George R. Sims, the writer of a famous column, 'Mustard and Cress', for *The Referee* was often a guest at Mill House. His pseudonym was 'Dagonet' and he collaborated with both Scott and Wilson Barrett to write plays, as well as his verses, of which 'Christmas Day at the Workhouse' is probably the best known. On one occasion Sims roamed around Overstrand having had the news spread abroad that he was a lunatic and that his companion, Henry Petit, was his keeper. On another occasion, he bought all the home-made blackberry jam from the hostess of Mill House, knowing that Scott was very partial to it and was due in a few days. Ghostly rattling and murderous cries around the lanes late at night could usually be attributed to Sims and his cronies.

It is not always clear who stayed at Mill House and who stayed elsewhere, though Mill House always had, at least, to be visited. Lady Battersea, wife of the prominent MP Cyril Flower, tells us of her visitors at The Pleasaunce. She recalled Sir George Alexander staying there, for instance, but it is probable that Scott first brought Overstrand to his attention. It seems that some of the famous names linked with Overstrand may only have visited once, but many did so on numerous occasions. The fact remains that it became a very fashionable place, a mecca for a number of folk in the public eye and as a consequence for many others besides.

The 'Poppyland' industry

Having mentioned the wide variety of Scott's writings, it is now time to concentrate on his publications that particularly refer to 'Poppyland', and some of the other publications that followed from other authors. The first article in the *Daily Telegraph* was the forerunner of a series directly related to Overstrand and Sidestrand, but places further afield were also covered, for instance Great Yarmouth and Lowestoft. A peculiar pattern seems to emerge from Scott's comparative style of writing in that one gains the feeling that Overstrand is preferred to Cromer, Cromer is in turn preferred to Great Yarmouth and so on! Perhaps it would be fairer to say that he tries to pick out the positive points in favour of each, though undoubtedly his preference is for the quieter places.

In due course his articles were collected together and published as books. The best known of these is that first published as *Poppy-land Papers*. It appeared in 1885 (bearing the date 1886) as a small, fine bound copy, published by Carson and Comerford and is naturally a very desirable collector's item today. (There have been two facsimile reprints in the 1990s, to meet demand, and collectors should be careful to distinguish these from originals.) It gives an insight, if slightly romanticised, into the area in the latter years of Victoria's reign. The local publishers, Jarrolds, realised that it was a very saleable booklet in East Anglia and by 1894 they had taken it on and it had reached its fourth edition, being bound now in a blue, hard cover with gold lettering and red poppies. The cover title has been reduced to *Poppy-land*, though *Poppy-land: Papers Descriptive of Scenery on the East Coast* is retained as the full heading inside. Curiously, all editions have eleven chapters of articles, all of which concern Cromer and Overstrand, except for two, one about Lowestoft and one about Great Yarmouth. Under the circumstances the balance of the booklet does not suit the title! However, it was sufficient to encourage the Grand Hotel at Lowestoft to take the first page for advertising, though any visitor coming to Lowestoft might be rather put out to realise how far away 'Poppyland' still was.

The editions of *Poppy-land Papers* are a little difficult to follow. A copy printed 'Fifteenth edition' on the title page has 'Fourth edition' printed on the cover, though the cover number may refer to the binding which is now of white card and giving the full title, but with the same poppy design. This edition is again published by Jarrolds, who presumably continued to publish the collection until demand ceased.

No doubt there was some manoeuvring regarding copyright going on when Hutchinson and Co published a collection of their own, *Blossomland and Falling*

Fashionable Cromer in the 1890s

Leaves, in 1890. As well as 'Poppyland' being dropped from the title, five of the chapters were omitted, but the total was increased to include thirty-one of Scott's articles in all. The 'Garden of Sleep' poem disappears from the front of the book to reappear in a full chapter entitled 'The Garden of Sleep'. The Overstrand chapters are spread through the book and continue to form the largest selection of eight articles, but as well as British places of interest, many articles on Continental resorts visited by Scott are included. The chapter entitled 'Among the Blossoms', written about Cobham, seems to provide the title for this edition; it is in this publication too that we find Scott saying that 'The Cromer that we visit now is not the Cromer I wrote about but a few short years ago as my beloved Poppyland'.

Scott having popularised the area, the people had come. With their coming came the development of something of a 'Poppyland' industry. The Great Eastern Railway took up the theme of 'Poppyland', and they produced many posters encouraging people to use their services to visit North Norfolk. Postcards were produced by the thousand. The majority featured the 'Tower' and the 'Garden of Sleep'. 'Poppyland' was no longer restricted (if it ever had been, bearing in mind the inclusion of Lowestoft and Great Yarmouth in *Poppy-land Papers*) to the area of Overstrand and Sidestrand. The postcard companies unashamedly overprinted pictures of the 'Tower' with town names. For their purposes the Tower was at Cromer, Sheringham and probably Mundesley as well.

Other publications on 'Poppyland' appeared. The artist Parsons Norman was commissioned to produce a series of pictures of the area for a book. Every view features a profusion of poppies. The text of this book, *Poppyland*, dwells on the delights of the area in a somewhat sugary manner. The copy in front of the present authors evidently once belonged to a far from impressed reader, for large sections of the text have been crossed out and the note, 'Most of the letterpress of this book consists of the most devastating sentimental tosh!' has been written at the foot of the first page.

The *Lady's Pictorial* dispatched one of its writers, Mrs Alfred Barlyn, together with an artist, W. W. Russell, to Overstrand to investigate the area for them. The resulting articles and pictures were reproduced in a book entitled *Vera in Poppyland*, a very enjoyable read. It is dedicated to 'My friend, Mr. Clement Scott' and dates probably from the mid-1890s, with the enjoyment coming from a very gentle 'send-up' of, not the area, but the fever that had infected 'Poppyland'. The four friends in the story enjoy the pleasures of Overstrand, constantly expecting to bump into someone rich or famous. Whenever something out of the ordinary occurs 'Great Scott!' is the expression that springs to their lips. One of the company becomes infatuated with the local rhyme:

Trimingham, Gimingham, Knapton and Trunch,
Southrepps and Northrepps lie all of a bunch.

which leads eventually to the enquiry as to whether the lines were written by Scott or Swinburne! The book's concluding chapter rather irreverently pictures a donkey in the 'Garden of Sleep' with the lines 'I am waiting for thee in the hush of the corn' beneath it.

Part of a Poppyland china service, made for Rounce and Wortley of Cromeer and Sheringham

It was not only in the field of publications that entrepreneurs sought to further their business by promoting 'Poppyland'. 'Poppyland' china was sold in local shops, from candleholders to full tea services. These have now become collector's items. Jarrolds, Rounce and Wortley and B. A. Watts of Sheringham all had china made featuring their own poppy designs. Another item produced was a miniature replica of the 'Tower' in the Garden of Sleep, and of course many souvenirs carried pictures of the 'Tower'.

Daniel Davison, a Cromer chemist and photographer, produced what was to become one of the most famous of the 'Poppyland' by-products, Poppyland Bouquet. This was principally a perfume, although soap was also made. The perfume was sold world-wide and made until 1930. It was based on a French spirit and used fifteen other ingredients. His shop in Jetty Street was an ideal spot for retailing these items and, as the picture on the back cover of this booklet shows, he featured it prominently in window displays.

The maid of the mill

With all the publicity that this corner of rural Norfolk suddenly received from the writings of Clement Scott, it is not surprising that at least one local character would emerge and become modestly famous. In this story it turned out to be the miller's daughter, Louie Jermy. Again, the stories vary in their detail, but to the end of her life in 1934 she constantly told her version of the first meeting with Scott at the gate to Mill House.

Her father, the miller, Alfred, was married four times, Marie Louisa being the eldest daughter of his first wife, Cecelia. She was born in 1864 in Tower Lane and so was 19 when she first met Clement Scott.

We must bring into the story here one of the chief sources of information on the life of Louie Jermy, the book *The Maid of the Mill*, compiled the year following Louie's death by Gwen Parry. This anthology brought together the memories of many who had visited or lived in Overstrand and who had met Louie. One must be careful when reading, for as with all reminiscences of this type, it is all too easy to fall into error on detail, and this certainly happened, as instanced by the date of Scott's death being given as 1912 instead of 1904. As we said at the outset, legend changes stories to give the desired effect, and humans being human, even those involved in events can do this; yet from these recollections we are able to draw a picture of a young girl who became part of a world quite different to the one in which she had grown up.

Louie was typical of Norfolk folk of the time. She was not very well educated, but was kind, generous and well-mannered. She was very able, particularly when it came to housework and cooking, and she thought nothing of digging up potatoes or plucking chickens. All this stood her in good stead for what was to follow, as the famous from the theatrical and literary professions began to arrive at Mill

House. And with Clement Scott as a frequent visitor for the next fifteen years, it was natural that there was a certain amount of local gossip about the relationship between him and Louie. David Henry discounts all such rumour when writing in *The Maid of the Mill*, and Clement always remained 'Mr Scott' to Louie.

'That hers was a striking personality', writes C. J. Barritt in the same publication, 'was apparent to all who ever had occasion to make her acquaintance. The marked individuality there shown was as much a part and picture of the time in which she lived as were the cliff-side home surroundings of holiday charm for the many who year after year came to know her and Poppyland.' J. Jefferson Farjeon perhaps goes deeper into her personality. 'I always felt, when talking to Louie, that she lived in a world largely borrowed from other minds. Her vivid imagination and her faculty for dramatisation, quickly achieved the necessary collaboration, causing her to become one with her part. In some form she must inevitably have expressed her particular vitality, but she became married to her imaginations and her associations, and it may be – though I am by no means sure of this – that she missed many more practical contacts through the glamour of her mental existence.'

Clara Watts-Dunton recalls that she tried to persuade Louie to accompany her to London, in service to herself. This Mrs Watts-Dunton was unable to do but Louie did occasionally venture to the capital to see theatrical performances. She did also spend a short time there in service, part of it, it seems, with the Scotts, and part as house-keeper to the family of Sir Edward Burne-Jones. He being an artist, she saw Rossetti, Whistler, Ruskin and others of that ilk, but while hearing them doubtless influenced her, it is difficult to imagine that she was satisfied in the position in which she found herself. After all, in 'Poppyland' she was the hostess herself and in one sense a celebrity as well. So, after a brief flirtation with London, Louie returned to her home.

G. R. Sims continued to write with emotion of Louie many years after Scott's death. By 1919 he was 72 and one of the last survivors of the original group of Scott's friends to visit 'Poppyland'. He recorded the fact that three years after the death of her father, Louie left Mill House. 'So snaps another link with the pleasant and picturesque past. Miss Jermy should write her reminiscences. She has been the guardian home from home angel of famous men.'

There is a curious connection for one of the present authors in the story at this point, for his great uncle, Fred Stibbons, was from 1909 a caddy at Cromer Golf Course. He was the author of a number of articles and verses published about the area. In one of his books, *In the King's Country*, he tells how he too was a twice-weekly visitor to 'Poppyland' House, as Mill House was by then called. He recalls Louie as 'taken all for all, the most remarkable woman I have met'. He also tells us that Louie had to leave the house in which she had become famous. Louie went to a cottage in Tower Lane, now gone over the edge of the cliff. She took with

◀ *Top left: the miller, Alfred Jermy. Top right: Louie Jermy in her younger years at Mill House. Bottom left: Louie Jermy at Tower Lane. Bottom right: The mill.*

her a few treasured mementoes of the heyday of Poppyland, including the faded 'Poppyland' fancy dress she had worn in her youth, and memories of the busy times at Mill House. She is remembered in the district in her later years, selling flowers and herbs door to door, and needing but little encouragement to speak of her memories. Finally, in 1934, she was laid to rest in the family grave in the corner of the churchyard, Sidestrand's new 'Garden of Sleep'.

Before and after Scott's visit

We must make some tentative assessment of the impact of the 'Poppyland' legend on North Norfolk. How much power did Scott wield in his pen? Was it the sea and countryside about which he wrote that brought others to see for themselves now that the railway had come? Or was it the love affair itself which he had with 'Poppyland' that attracted so many? Simplifying the question, without Scott, would the area have become so popular?

Overstrand in 1863 contained two private citizens worthy of mention in Harrod's Directory and nine names are given in the commercial section. Four are farmers, two shopkeepers, and the others are a shoemaker, the parish clerk and a publican. The population in total was 253 in the census of 1861. True, not far away were Northrepps Cottage and the Gurneys, whose family had brought a select popularity to Cromer in the 1790s, and the town already warranted a substantial entry in the Directory. Kelly's directory in 1879 gives 21 private entries and 112 commercial for Cromer, but Overstrand still has only 12 in total and the population had increased to 266 by 1871.

However, reference to Kelly's directory for 1892 tells a very different story. The population of Overstrand has reached 443 and there are 22 private and 32 commercial entries. Of these, 17 are lodging houses, with even the bricklayer and road surveyor offering apartments with a good sea view. The population and commercial development of Cromer shows a rise of similar proportions in the same time. True, the railway had reached Cromer in 1877 and a second line had arrived in 1887, but it is difficult to attribute the meteoric rise in popularity of the towns and villages just to improved accessibility. True, also, that many of the names listed are of people who were already resident in 1879 and who have gained inclusion by virtue of offering lodgings, but further research would doubtless show this to be a small part of the whole. The third factor that must be admitted is the general increase in popularity in 'taking the waters' that occurred throughout the country in late Victorian times, but while that may account for the attraction of such places as Southend and resorts near to London, it still required time and initiative to make the journey to Cromer.

Another aspect of change is seen through study of the building carried out, particularly in Overstrand, in the late eighties and nineties. It seems that Cyril Flower, Lord Battersea, would have built locally anyway, possibly at Sheringham,

Overstrand, 1981, with The Pleasaunce in the centre of the photograph ▶

but his acquisition of two adjoining properties at Overstrand, at the suggestion of Lord Suffield, was in 1888 and therefore in the 'Poppyland' era. These two properties were referred to as his cottage, and christened by one of his visitors 'The Pleasaunce'. To the cottage came Princess Louise, and Clement Scott wrote that she 'actually took her tea on the wee lawns and nobody ever turned their heads to look at her. That the fishermen's wives hung their washing up in full view . . . and the Royal visitor bought her own stamps at the shop and strolled unattended on the sand – this seems incredible.' The Princess was but one among many visitors, and when he was elevated to the peerage Lord Battersea, finding he had more opportunity to be at Overstrand, decided that The Pleasaunce must be improved. He employed Edwin Lutyens, then early in a famous career, as architect and The Pleasaunce became the building it is today. Overstrand was on its way to gaining the nickname 'The Village of Millionaires'.

We might pause with Lady Battersea for a moment as she describes from where many of the lodging houses of Overstrand had come. 'During the season the inhabitants live in strange little makeshift dwellings, even in railway carriages, standing at the rear of their houses, the latter having been given over to lodgers.' She and Lord Battersea created in the grounds of The Pleasaunce a second Overstrand garden that became as famous as the first. Ellen Thorneycroft Fowler was to look back on this garden as a 'Garden of Dreams'. She compares it to something out of the *Arabian Nights* for its variety and abundance.

The question we are considering is Scott's influence on the area, and we must obviously note that Lord and Lady Battersea were also very influential through their connections. One of the next major buildings again had Lutyens as architect, as Lord Hillingdon engaged him to design Overstrand Hall. This too was to be a grand building with beautiful grounds. Sir George Lewis, a famous lawyer, also bought land and engaged Lutyens, but in the end opted to purchase a Danish-style house complete from an exhibition in Paris. Sir George Alexander and Sir Squire Bancroft, already mentioned as from the theatrical world, both expressed interest in Lutyens' services, but although the former bought land, neither ever put building in hand.

Another building towards which Scott contributed is the Roman Catholic church in Cromer. When staying in Poppyland, Scott wrote to the Bishop of Northampton, then the diocesan bishop for the whole of the east of England, urging him to make arrangements for a place of worship for Roman Catholics on holiday. It is therefore appropriate that the memorial to Scott is so close to the church. Scott's letter is on view in the church hall.

Space precludes full mention of all the other properties built at Overstrand about the turn of the century, so a brief summary must suffice. Carrwood House was built for Sir Henry Fowler, Lord Wolverhampton, and The Grange for actor Sir John Hare. He found life in Overstrand too dull and it was acquired by Mr Player of cigarette fame.

The retired headmaster of Eton, Rev Edward Lyttleton, was resident at Grangegorman, and Sea Marge was built for Sir Edgar Speyer. Winston Churchill was staying nearby at Pear Tree Cottage in 1914 and is reputed to have mobilised the fleet using the Sea Marge telephone, and then to have been responsible for the expulsion of Sir Edgar from the country as an alien! Meadow Cottage, owned by the Macmillan family, and Corner House (now known as Danum House), later home of authoress Florence Barclay, must be mentioned as well.

The building of hotels was a natural result of the coming of visitors. This affected Cromer and Sheringham more than Overstrand, though the Overstrand Hotel was built in this era and there were major hotels built in Mundesley, the Royal being the first. The Grand, Marlborough, Metropole, Cliftonville and the rebuilt de Paris at Cromer all come into this period, as do Cromer Pier (opened 1901) and many of the amenities provided by Cromer Urban District Council. It is a truism to say that had the visitors not come, many of the amenities would not have been needed, but such general advantages to the town as the new fire station and cemetery were paid for indirectly as the ratepayers could frequently make enough money from their visitors to improve their own lot.

While it can be seen that there were many factors that contributed to the open-ing up of North Norfolk to tourists, it must be said that without Scott it is unlikely that it would have been on the same scale. True, the railways saw potential in driving through to Cromer, and the first decade of the new century saw them going further in opening the 'Poppy Line' from Cromer to Mundesley. But without Scott would the volume of traffic have been generated? If not Scott, could anyone else have fired the interest of London? We think not, for we have already argued that in this time he was one of the most influential of writers, and whether respected, feared or disliked, he was certainly one of whom note was taken. His influence combined the middle class who read his articles and the theatrical and artistic world in his own circle of friends. The combination of the two involved many people.

In retrospect then it is possible to build up a strong case to say that Scott had a remarkable influence on North Norfolk. From a nearer viewpoint this influence was not appreciated. The *North Norfolk News*, in its edition of 12th September 1909, reports the proceedings at Cromer Council. The Secretary to the Metropolitan Drinking Fountain and Cattle Trough Association, one Captain Smith, had written again to the Council concerning the siting of a 'fountain', a memorial to the late Clement Scott. The council was far from unanimous in supporting its coming to Cromer, and one member suggested it had been 'hurled at them'. Another member doubted that it should be referred to as a fountain when in fact it was a cattle drinking trough. 'Unfortunately,' said Captain Smith in his letter, 'the fountain and trough has already been despatched, with the inscription placed on it.' Suffice to say that the drinking-trough is referred to locally as 'The Fountain' and can be seen today at the entrance to 'Poppyland', at the junction of Overstrand and Northrepps Roads.

The decline of 'Poppyland'

This might be a misleading title for it implies the decline of the area. Its appeal has certainly changed, without necessarily declining. What we are concerned with is the fading of the 'Poppyland' story, the ending of many of the elements that made up this era in the history of this corner of Norfolk. The poppies still bloom, some years in abundance and some years sparsely, for their seeds are very long lived and can lie many years dormant below the ground, to be reactivated when disturbed and brought back into contact with warmth and moisture; but few of the direct links with Scott's 'Poppyland' remain.

The people of Sidestrand often discussed when the tower would finally topple over the edge of the cliff. One morning in 1916 the villagers had looked and seen the tower, on the cliff-top. At midday, two villagers arrived having walked from Cromer and reported that the tower had gone. Gradually the graveyard too slipped away and the bones sticking out of the cliff were a morbid attraction, along with the stones of the tower on the beach.

Writing in 1912 Mr Percy Lindley, a contributor to the Great Eastern Railway house magazine, suggested that the 'Poppyland' era had already ended. He stated

Tower Lane, looking back from the edge of the cliff with Louie's cottage on the right.

in a GER book *On the East Coast* that 'golf is to Cromer now what the Garden of Sleep was in early days' and he talks of 'the late regal red poppy'. This was undoubtedly a premature obituary for although Scott was dead, Sims occasionally brought 'Poppyland' to the fore, and as we have said, the souvenir trade was in full swing. The First World War ended the great days of 'Poppyland', but business remained brisk between the wars. Louie Jermy's death was the last fling of those directly involved in the story, and the Second World War saw the end of many, though by no means all, of the large hotels. They did not survive their occupation by the military. The Overstrand Hotel was already dangerously near the cliff edge and the wartime mining and later the clearing of these mines did not help the stability of the cliffs. A new hotel company soon found itself in difficulties and then a fire gutted the building in 1949. The site was cleared and eventually the foundations fell into the sea. Two years later the Danish Pavilion was largely destroyed by fire. The owner turned the remaining section into a motel. 'The Pleasaunce', 'Overstrand Hall' and 'Sea Marge' have survived but have passed from private family ownership into corporate hands.

Sidestrand Hall also passed to the County after housing troops and then Methodist holidaymakers. Sidestrand Church has seen over 100 years pass since it was moved back from the cliff-top; Overstrand had its own St Martin's church

Tower Lane in 1981. The cottages stood to the left, the old church tower about 300 yards into the picture.

restored in 1914 when it took over again from the smaller Christ Church that Scott knew.

At the time of writing the first edition of this booklet in 1981 a sprinkling of house names in Overstrand and Cromer seemed to be all that recalled 'Poppyland', although the 'Poppyland Tearooms' on the promenade at Cromer could be recalled in the previous decade. With the reorganisation of local government in the 1970s, it was suggested that what is now called 'North Norfolk District Council' be called 'Poppyland District Council', but the suggestion evidently did not strike a chord with councillors at the time. Perhaps it had all faded a little too far into the past. Suffice it to say that our own publishers, specialising in the field of local history, felt it a name that they could perpetuate.

The visitor who walks past Overstrand, by that section of road whose straightness gives away the fact that it too is an addition to the old coast road, can come to the Mill House on his left and peer over a gate to the house. Behind him is the rising ground on which the mill itself stood. If he travels on towards Sidestrand, he will notice a seat in memory of Louie Jermy on the right and Tower Lane going off to the left. It is, as we have said, difficult to imagine that this was the main road. Walking down it one comes to the cliff edge. There, staring down to the beach below, looking around to some of the spectacular falls of cliff, it is

A mysterious new tower appeared in Poppyland in 1984. Gravestones and tower came and went in the course of a few days' filming, and bathing machines returned to Cromer beach for a day.
Below: Alan Howard as Clement Scott.

again hard to picture on the left, some 20 or 30 feet from the present cliff edge, the cottage where Louie ended her days. Off to the right, 300 yards to the east, stood the tower, in the midst of the 'Garden of Sleep'. The final mystery of this story comes with these lines. They seem appropriate to that spot on the cliff-top, but their author, who matched Scott's original romanticism, is unknown to us.

> It has passed to the deep with its poppies of red,
> Away on the cliffs desolation is spread,
> For the tower in ruins that guarded their sleep
> Has passed with the poppies away to the deep.
> I sigh as I look far away o'er the sea,
> And I think of the day that alas! ne'er can be.

Postscript

Twenty years have passed since the first edition of this booklet in 1981. Since then, there has been a 'Poppyland' revival in many ways, in which we trust that our publishers and we can claim a part. The visitor will see the name 'Poppyland' in use in many places around north Norfolk. In our modern age 'branding' is very important in the market place – a concept of which Scott seems to have been well aware!

1983 marked the centenary of Scott's first visit and 29th August provided the opportunity to take part in a celebratory walk along the route that Scott took. Once again the local press carried stories of 'Poppyland', the *Daily Telegraph* recalled its part in the tale and the *Today* programme began with a brief mention of the occasion. Many locals and visitors gathered at the site of the now demolished Cromer High station, and walked to the clifftops by Cromer lighthouse. They followed the path by the golf links to walk into Overstrand before turning inland to follow the road for the final few yards to Mill House.

Holkham Pottery created a special mug to celebrate the one hundred years and for the month of August the window of Jarrolds' shop in Cromer featured an abundance of poppies, alongside our companion publication *Poppyland in Pictures*, which evokes through a selection of pictures from those late Victorian times the landscape and scenes that greeted Scott.

The greatest publicity of all was at the beginning of 1985 when the BBC transmitted the film *Poppyland*. Four and a half million homes shared the story, written for television by William Humble, and produced by Richard Broke. The latter's family connection with Mill House and the desire to make a film of the story coincided with our visit to Mill House when researching this booklet. The many months of preparation required finally came to fruition with the commencement of filming in June 1984. Alan Howard played Scott and Phoebe Nicholls, Louie.

Director John Madden and cameraman Nat Crosby led the team that faced the inclement weather Norfolk provided!

In so many ways the resulting film provided a marvellous reflection of the original 'Poppyland' era, from the characterisations of the cast through to the music, developed by George Fenton from the Isidore de Lara 'Garden of Sleep' theme. And what did the critics make of the film? Virtually without exception it was praised in all aspects. We rather think that Scott would have been pleased! He would probably have reviewed it at considerable length, in a very 'picturesque' style!

The critic of the television trade magazine *Broadcast* called it 'the year's delight' and went on to say 'this film might do for Poppyland what the Victorian trendies did all over again'. We hope that by whatever means you heard of 'Poppy-land' you've enjoyed reading of it and suggest a visit to Cromer Museum, a walk by Mill House to a now very overgrown Tower Lane and a little relaxation of the imagination into a time gone by! And of course you can now join us at www.poppyland.co.uk – though we suspect that is something that Scott would have liked to escape from at times!